Pablo Picasso

Published by The Child's World®
1980 Lookout Drive • Mankato, MN 56003-1705
800-599-READ • www.childsworld.com

Acknowledgments
The Child's World®: Mary Berendes, Publishing Director
Red Line Editorial: Editorial direction and production
The Design Lab: Design

Photographs ©: Francis G. Mayer/Corbis, cover, 7; AP Images,
5; Public Domain, 9 (top), 9 (bottom), 13; Museo Picasso/The
Bridgeman Art Library, 10; Library of Congress, 12–13; Art
Resource, NY, 14, 15, 18–19; Alexander Burkatovski/Corbis,
17; Bettmann/Corbis, 20

ISBN 9781626873537
LCCN 2014930692

Printed in the United States of America
Mankato, MN
July, 2014
PA02223

Cover Image Credits:
Large Still Life on a Pedestal Table, 1931 © 2013 Estate of Pablo Picasso /
Artists Rights Society (ARS), New York

ABOUT THE AUTHOR

Darice Bailer is the author of many books for young readers. She has won a Parents' Choice Gold Award and a Parents' Choice Approved Seal for her work.

ABOUT THE ILLUSTRATOR

J.T. Morrow has worked as a freelance illustrator for more than 25 years and has won several awards. His work has appeared in advertisements, on packaging, in magazines, and in books. He lives near San Francisco, California, with his wife and daughter.

CONTENTS

CHAPTER 1

The Boy Who Liked to Draw

Pablo Picasso was one of the most famous artists of the 1900s. He was a very talented painter. He also made collages, **sculptures**, and pottery. For hundreds of years, artists painted things the way they looked. Pablo used his imagination and created new **modern** art.

When Pablo was a child in the 1880s, all he wanted to do was draw. Sometimes the family's maid had to drag the boy to school. Pablo's maid could make him go to class. But that didn't mean he was going to listen! When it was math time, Pablo drew pictures with numbers. He wrote 7 upside down and drew a big nose!

PICASSO'S NAME

Most Spanish people use the last names of their parents' families. The last name of Pablo's father was Ruiz Blasco and his mother's was Picasso López. At first Pablo called himself Pablo Ruiz y Picasso. Later he signed his paintings as simply Picasso.

Pablo Picasso created many famous works of art.

Pablo had a big imagination. And all Pablo wanted to do was draw. On weekends his father took him to art museums. Maybe Pablo could copy Spanish painters and become a famous artist. At first Pablo painted like the **masters**—the experts he saw in museums. But then he came up with his own ideas.

Pablo invented new styles of art. His drawings, paintings, and sculptures did not always look like real people or things. No one had ever seen art like it before. Pablo used all blue paint for a few years. Then he painted in light pinks or rose instead. Later Pablo dreamed up a whole new way of painting with different shapes. Artists saw that they didn't have to paint like artists had in the past. They could create new ways to express themselves.

> A still life? It doesn't look very still to me!

Pablo Picasso created many famous works of art. Picasso's work revealed the artist's big imagination.

CHAPTER 2
Winning Awards

Pablo Picasso was born in Málaga, Spain, on October 25, 1881. When Pablo was one year old, he picked up one of his dad's pencils. The Spanish word for pencil is *lapiz*. "Piz!" Pablo cried. Pencil was his first word! The little toddler began to draw.

When he was older, Pablo took art classes at the school where his father taught. Pablo drew with a pencil or pen. He painted with watercolor or oil paint. He liked using different kinds of art supplies. He was always experimenting.

When Pablo was 13, his father took a new job teaching art in Barcelona. Barcelona is a big city on the northern coast of Spain. Pablo's father liked the **traditional** way Spanish artists had been painting. Some of their **portraits** were dark, but the pictures were like real photographs. But in Barcelona, artists were interested in new painting ideas from Paris. A French painter named Georges-Pierre Seurat used tiny dabs of bright paint. Other artists were trying new things with their brushes.

Old Spanish masters including Diego Velázquez made realistic paintings (detail, left). Georges-Pierre Seurat used dots of paint to create a whole scene (detail, right).

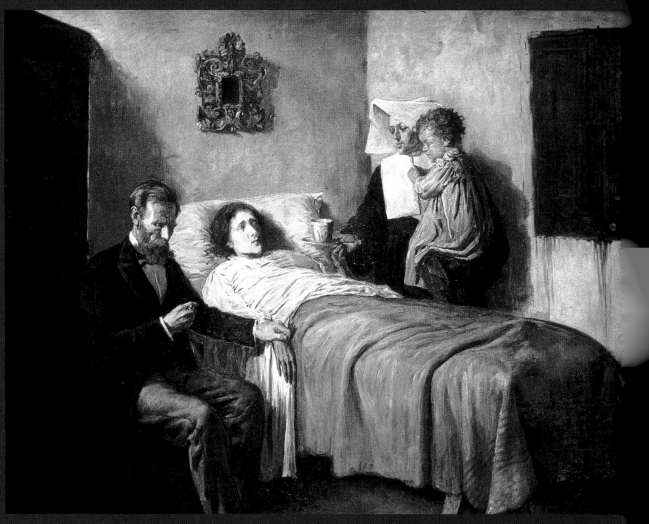

Science and Charity shows Pablo's skill at a young age.

When Pablo was 15, his uncle asked him to paint a picture of his Aunt Pepa. As the story goes, Pablo finished it in less than an hour. Then his father **posed** for another painting. Pablo's father pretended to be a doctor sitting next to a sick woman. Pablo drew a nun holding a child and offering the sick woman a drink of water. When Pablo finished the painting, it had the touch of an older, experienced artist. It could have hung in a museum. It didn't look as though someone who was just 15 could have painted it. In 1897, the painting, *Science and Charity*, won an award in a show.

Pablo was making a name for himself. He started going to the best art school in Spain. The teachers showed him how to paint the way his dad had taught him. Pablo quit school. He wanted to create a new style of his own. He would teach himself how to paint a new way.

PLAYING WITH PERSPECTIVE

Artists usually drew trees and houses smaller if they were far away. And they painted things larger if they were close by. This is called **perspective**. *It is the way things look in a camera. But in the 1880s, French painter Paul Cézanne made a painting with the houses and landscape all the same size. Later, Pablo would make paintings showing more than one perspective at the same time.*

CHAPTER 3

Shocking the Art World

When Picasso was 18, one of his paintings, *Les Derniers Moments (The Last Times)*, was chosen for the 1900 World's Fair in Paris. At the fair, countries showed what their people had invented, like talking movies and escalators. They also displayed art. Picasso's painting was going to hang in the Spanish **pavilion**. Thousands of people would see it.

Paris was a beautiful city. Artists kept experimenting with new ways of painting. There were many famous art museums, such as the Louvre. Paris was the art capital of the world. Picasso decided to move to Paris. There he visited the museums. He made friends with other artists.

The city of Paris, 1890s

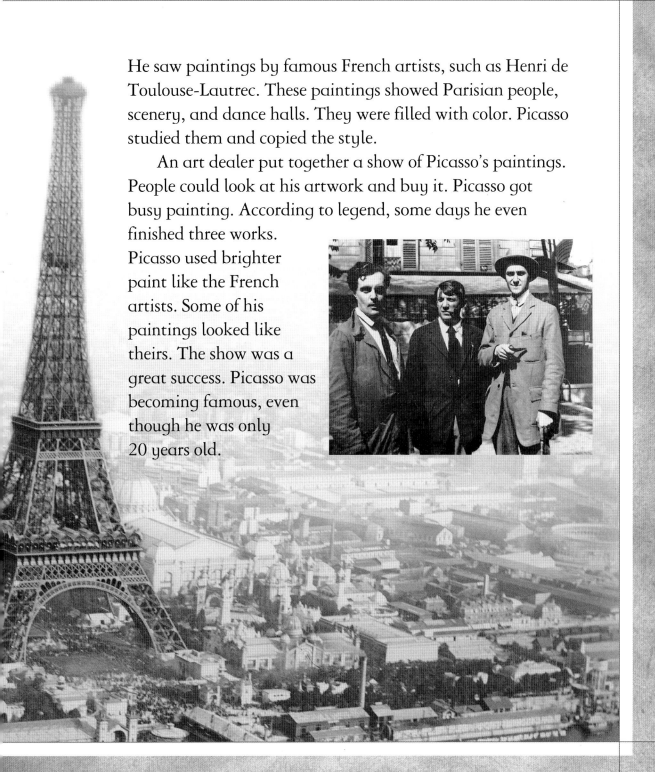

He saw paintings by famous French artists, such as Henri de Toulouse-Lautrec. These paintings showed Parisian people, scenery, and dance halls. They were filled with color. Picasso studied them and copied the style.

An art dealer put together a show of Picasso's paintings. People could look at his artwork and buy it. Picasso got busy painting. According to legend, some days he even finished three works. Picasso used brighter paint like the French artists. Some of his paintings looked like theirs. The show was a great success. Picasso was becoming famous, even though he was only 20 years old.

Picasso (center) made friends with many artists in Paris, including the famous modern artist Amedeo Modigliani (left).

Then, a friend of Picasso's died in 1901. Over the next three years, Picasso painted many pictures of sad people. The paintings were in shades of blue that made the pictures dark and gloomy. The paintings showed how unhappy he was. This time became known as his Blue Period.

In 1904, Picasso moved into a neighborhood on a hill in Paris. It was called Montmartre, and many artists lived there. Picasso and his friends liked to go to the circus there. Picasso began painting the clowns and jugglers. His friends encouraged him.

The Old Guitarist, late 1903–early 1904 © 2013 Estate of Pablo Picasso / Artists Rights Society (ARS), New York

Picasso felt happier and used rose-colored paint. The paintings were brighter. One day, Picasso drew a family of acrobats. The painting is called the *Family of Saltimbanques*. *Saltimbanques* is a French word for clowns. Picasso tells a story of a

The Old Guitarist *is one of the most famous Blue Period pieces.*

circus family in his painting. The performers look as though they are traveling to a new show. They have only the circus clothes they're wearing and what they're carrying. There's nothing in the landscape either. Picasso doesn't show one tree or house. Everyone looks a little sad. The painting hangs in the National Gallery of Art in Washington, DC. It's one of Picasso's most famous paintings from his Rose Period.

Family of Saltimbanques brings out many different emotions in its viewers.

Picasso was a young artist in a new century. Life was changing for him and the world. Picasso wanted to throw out the old rules of painting. He wanted to come up with a new style. Picasso saw African statues and masks in a Paris museum. They would inspire him to mix an old style with a new one.

In 1906, Picasso painted a picture of a friend, Gertrude Stein. She was an American writer who lived in Paris. Stein had bought some of his paintings. Picasso thought about the masks he'd seen. He painted Stein's face like a wooden mask.

In 1907, Picasso met the French painter Georges Braque. They became friends and inspired each other. Braque was painting scenery with different shapes. The houses looked like stacks of brown blocks. Picasso thought about using shapes as well. In 1909, Picasso painted a little town on top of a hill. He experimented with shape the way Braque did. Picasso called one painting *Houses on a Hill* and another *The Reservoir*. The rooftops in his paintings look like rectangles or triangles. A house looks like a cube. This new style of painting is called **cubism**.

CUBISM COLLAGES

In 1912, Picasso glued printed paper on his paintings and began making collages. Painters hadn't made collages before. Picasso's first collage is called Still Life with Chair Caning. *This painting from 1912 started a new style of cubism. It was more colorful and decorative.*

CHAPTER 4
An Artist All Life Long

In 1917, Picasso designed the scenery and costumes for a ballet. While working on the ballet, he met a Russian ballerina. Her name was Olga Kokhlova. In 1918, Picasso married Kokhlova, and they had a baby boy. The couple named the baby Paulo.

In 1924, Picasso painted a picture of Paulo as a clown. He called it *Paulo as Harlequin*. A harlequin is a clown. Picasso was painting in a style more like people were used to, but only for a while.

In 1927, Picasso fell in love with a woman named Marie-Thérèse Walter, and Olga left. Walter and Picasso had a daughter, Maya. Picasso drew a picture of Maya in *The Artist's Daughter with a Boat*. But Picasso didn't paint her eyes where they should go. He painted them far off to the side. And her nose and lips weren't in the right place either. He did the same thing in other paintings. Picasso didn't paint exactly what he saw. He used a little imagination.

In 1937, Germany bombed the Spanish town of Guernica. It was a small town near Barcelona. The town was destroyed and many people died. Picasso expressed his sadness in a famous painting titled *Guernica*. Picasso's

Guernica was shown at
the Paris World's Fair.
The people and animals
almost looked like
cartoons. But you could
see the pain and suffering
in their faces. *Guernica*
became one of the most
famous paintings of
the century.

SCULPTURE

*Picasso made many unusual
sculptures during his life. He used
whatever he found lying around
to make sculptures of animals or
people. In 1951, Picasso took
two little toy cars. He used one of
the cars for a baboon's face. The
windows became the eyes. The hood
became the nose!*

*Guernica captured the way many people felt about
war in black, white, and gray colors.*

After World War II ended in 1945, Picasso began living in the south of France. He tried pottery and sculpture. He became a great sculptor as well as a great painter. Sometimes he made sculptures out of junk. He kept making art as he grew older.

On April 8, 1973, Picasso died at age 91. He had looked at people in new ways. He saw them—and drew them—differently. He dared to create art that looked weird to some people. Yet it was bold and new and transformed art in the new century. Picasso helped introduce cubism and modern art. Artists who came after him felt free to create their own

Picasso displayed a bronze statue of a goat at a Paris art exhibit in 1952.

new styles. Picasso showed them that they didn't have to paint the way everybody else did. Picasso changed his style many times. No other artist came up with so many new ideas. Or changed as many times!

Picasso created more than 50,000 paintings, drawings, prints, sculptures, and pottery pieces. He was one of the greatest artists of the twentieth century.

Glossary

cubism (CUE-bizm) Cubism is an art style with many shapes and angles so that people and objects do not look real. Pablo Picasso invented cubism with a French artist named Georges Braque and introduced it to the world.

masters (MASS-turs) Masters are experts. Pablo Picasso liked to go to the art museums in Paris and study the masters' paintings there.

modern (MOD-urn) Modern is new or having to do with the present or recent past. Picasso stopped painting the way his father taught him and created modern art.

pavilion (puh-VIL-yuhn) A pavilion is a building that is used for an exhibit. Spain showed one of Picasso's paintings inside its pavilion at the 1900 World's Fair.

perspective (per-SPECK-tiv) Painting in perspective is giving a flat image an appearance of distance and depth. Paul Cézanne taught Pablo Picasso that he could ignore perspective and paint things all the same size.

portraits (POR-trits) Portraits are pictures of a person's face. Pablo's father showed him old Spanish portraits hanging in museums.

posed (POHZD) Someone who posed held a position. Picasso's father posed for a painting for Picasso.

sculptures (SKUHLP-churs) Sculptures are things that are carved and shaped out of stone, clay, wood, or other materials. Picasso made sculptures out of things he found.

traditional (truh-DISH-uhn-ul) Traditional relates to a custom or idea that has been passed down through the years. The traditional style of Spanish painting could be seen in the great museums around the country.

To Learn More

BOOKS

Jacobson, Rick. *Picasso: Soul on Fire*. Plattsburgh, NY: Tundra Books of Northern New York, 2011.

Winter, Jonah. *Just Behave, Pablo Picasso!* New York: Arthur A. Levine Books, 2012.

WEB SITES

Visit our Web site for links about Pablo Picasso:

childsworld.com/links

Note to Parents, Teachers, and Librarians:

We routinely verify our Web links to make sure they are safe and active sites. So encourage your readers to check them out!

Index